Book 1

in the series

"Her Story"

A Womanist Perspective

on Mary

Previously published as
Her Story: A Womanist Perspective on Mary
by Ermelinda Makkimane

(ermelindamakkimane@gmail.com)

Other books in the series, "Her Story":

Contents

Preface

A story like Mary's from the New Testament, fertile material for an imaginative retelling, wouldn't you say? There's so much written on Mary. Yet, here I am hoping my presentation is unique, is noticed. That's my audacious attempt then. To write *Mary's* version of events. To offer the twenty-first century reader a glimpse *into* her mind, her unique personality.

Drawing on scraps of information in the Gospels and the Book of the Acts of the Apostles, I have painted the picture of a woman of her time, deeply bound by the societal norms of the age, whose one single decision taken as a teenager would change the history of humankind. In this effort, I have tried to present a woman-centric, inward-looking perspective. Any blemishes therefore are owing to my own limited vision and should not be ascribed to the person I am trying to depict.

Read her story to find out for yourself.

Ermelinda Makkimane

Divar, Goa

July 2020

"Behold the handmaid of the Lord,"

"May God's will be done unto me."

Prologue

I look back, though back is not enough
for sometimes, I have to run forward
like Zacchaeus[1], and sometimes,
my present is melded in my past.
So I ponder, time is of no essence,
since I've reached timelessness,
less of a place and more a space
of boundlessness, abundance, overflowing.
From here which is also my there,
I tell my story.

Part 1

"Behold the handmaid of the Lord,"

"May God's will be done unto me."

How do I explain myself

being both reviled and blessed by generations?

I am the handmaid of the Lord,

I said, to the angel[2].

(Of course, I couldn't have *known* the angel)

The one who gave me the weird message.

Not something one would grasp immediately.

My response was naturally organic:

we were taught to show subservience

in matters pertaining to the divine.

So I did.

Little did I know how literally

the Lord would take me.

"But I am a virgin,"

I protested,

pregnant without knowing a man.

Unthinkable! Impossible!

The raveling and unraveling

of this has taken me a lifetime.

And still, I find no answer to the first 'how'

I asked that day. A sign was given,

I went, curious to confirm

and Elizabeth[3] was, giddily enough,

pregnant! I had never been close

to anyone, and yet when I saw her,

I remembered the angel's words:

"In her old age, has she conceived."

And I rejoiced for her, with her

for her barrenness had brought much misery.

But she confessed, it's not easy,

I get palpitations and can barely sleep at night.

My knees used to hurt.

Now they tremble as I begin to rise or sit.

I don't go out much; they point fingers at me,

the children, and the adults stop talking

when I pass by as if I have done some wrong.

I slowly digested what she told me,

when suddenly she's startled,

It kicked, the baby's moving!

I placed my hand where she guided me,

and I too felt the strong vibration.

We laughed and cried together.
I tried to make it easier for her
but I had no experience and the final days
were the most difficult. She needed
two people to help her rise.
And her husband's muteness didn't help either.
The midwife came only towards the end
of her long and difficult delivery.

And soon it was time for me to return.
My stomach had begun to show.
Elizabeth blessed me and sent me off.

Back home it was my turn
to get the cold-shoulder,
the not-so-soft sniggers.
They pointed me out wherever I went.
I couldn't understand why
the Lord would want me to experience this.
What child was this? Whose child?
Joseph[4] got to know. They came and told me
he was willing to divorce me privately
but then he changed his mind.

He told me much later about his dream:
how an angel had helped him arrive
at the right decision.
We didn't talk much, he loved his solitude
as I did mine. Sometimes he was so distant.
But he did seem to understand my travails.
For he made sure that I didn't have to carry
the water jugs back from the well.

He was passionate about his work,
engrossed in measuring and planing.
putting things together was easy for him.
Things were going on as per a set routine
when the announcement by Caesar Augustus
threw us into a quandary.
We would have to travel to Bethlehem
to complete our Citizenship registration,
it was the decree. We were the only ones
from Nazareth to go.
On a borrowed donkey
who was more bones than flesh,
we began the tedious journey.
With a very active baby almost due.

sitting on that donkey was torture,

but Joseph would not let me walk.

He fed the donkey lovingly and the animal

thrived under his care.

He, the donkey and me - we

reached Bethlehem late one night.

I was drenched with perspiration.

Halting at the nearest inn, Joseph went in

to find us a place, while the donkey and I,

we waited outside, sleepy, tired and hungry.

He came out almost as soon as he had entered:

There was no room. Chaos. Tempers running high.

Joseph was not a pushy man,

he said he'd ask ahead.

He tried to get me on to the donkey

but I indicated that I would rather walk.

How could I tell him about the searing pains

tearing through me every few minutes?

I threw one arm around the creature's head:

sensing my need, it stiffened its muscles

while I half dragged myself behind Joseph.

At every inn we stopped that night
they sent us further, quoting no room;
some had even put up signs that said:
"No rooms! Do not pester!"

We shuffled forward, feet caked in road dust.
When the spasms struck I could barely
lift my feet, my thighs seemed to have
hot wires running down them.
By then perspiration (or tears?)
had blinded me completely. Suddenly
I noticed a strong hand supporting me.
Then another on the other side.
They half lifted, half dragged me to a poorly lit barn

Was this an ambush? Part of the divine plan?
What God wanted a child to be born thus and thus?
That thought was uppermost as I sank
into a makeshift bed of hay, no cloth covering it either.
Someone dabbed at my face, I was able to see.
Two women were wordlessly working around me.

Joseph? Where was he? In the mouth
of this cave like barn,
I saw his silhouette, still and pensive.
was he wondering like me: what God? What child?
Another spasm of pain tore through me
jolting my upper body as my fingers dug
into the underside of my thighs,
a primeval posture. A warm compress
pressed down on me as I felt a warm trickle release.
What was this? The woman peering down
pressed at my abdomen as another wrenching pain
left me breathless and my legs trembling like jelly.
I felt a whoosh… And there was the child.
When my legs gained some semblance of dignity,
I looked for my precious babe, curious to see
what wonderous form was wrought in my being.
The younger woman had put him in a trough
and cleansed him of the blood while the older one
deftly cleaned me up. They spoke no word,
None was needed. The babe's first cry
had roused Joseph from his deep reverie.

And when the women had laid me in fresh hay

They brought the babe to me in swaddling.

My breasts had hung heavy through these last days,

now opened of their own volition.

And this tiny, helpless infant started rooting

It was a funny sight and everyone was asmiling.

even Joseph. The donkey too, it seemed to me,

but I couldn't be sure.

Part 2

Living in Nazareth had its own set of problems
for one, they never let me forget the fact
that Joseph was only an adoptive father.
And they didn't let him forget that too.
Him, my son, whose birth, angels heralded
to shepherds. They told us so
when they visited. Though I was not entirely comfortable
with their visit. Most Levitical Jews
would never be found in their vicinity.
I always wondered about this facet
of my faith that allowed for differences
in treatment meted out to fellow beings.

Still being back at home was much better
than running off to and living in Egypt.
What child was this on whose account
Joseph and I had endured such hardships?
He seemed so bright, and obedient,
ever willing to learn
the trade from his excellent father.
I watched them, father and son,
spend hours working together,
chatting even, exchanging ideas.

Joseph's eyes would glow with pride
as his foster son displayed
all the mastery of a budding carpenter.
He always cautioned the boy
while using nails; how ironical
that turned out later.

Joseph left too soon, I felt;
his quiet presence had been
comforting and I wondered
how we would manage,
yet my son took things in his stride
and ably took over the workshop.

Seeing him at work
I sometimes wondered,
had I dreamt it all up,
the angel? the shepherds?
What was I seeking?
And then he'd look up from his work
and smile at me
and I would forget
what I had been thinking.

And smile my fears away.

The initial heady days
after his birth, a time replete
with divine signs
was replaced with
emptiness and sometimes, just words,
"Didn't you know that I
would be going about
my Father's business?"
Marriage was not
on his agenda,
so the neighbors gossiped
about the carpenter's son
born to Mary.
It didn't help that he
chose to denounce
the people of Nazareth
publicly in the synagogue one day.
They forced him out
and would have thrown
him down a cliff
but he walked away, unhurt.

Just before he left
to begin his ministering
to the people,
I had learnt to weave seamlessly –
But before I finished
a seamless tunic for him,
he was gone.
I had always sensed
that a separation
was imminent.
I had just no inkling
of the form it would take.

Did a shiver pass through my body
when I swaddled him as a baby?
And then later remember doing the same
on a darkening evening drenched in tears.
Was there any warning?
Didn't Simeon's prophecy cause a shiver
to run down my spine? A sword will pierce
your heart, he had said! What utter lack of tact
by the revered old man, I had thought then.

In hindsight, I realize, no tact is better than
emotional torture.

What do you say to your son
who refuses to acknowledge you
in front of a crowd? Throwing lofty words,
seemingly at me, *Whosoever does the will
of the Father is my mother, my brother, my sister.*
I walked away, confused and hurt.

His cousins accompanying me
were too distressed to speak.
John, one of his disciples, followed me
and brought me the message
that my son would be in the hills that night.
So I set out, hope building up again.
This time I was not disappointed.

The first thing he said to me,
"Didn't you know I was referring to you?
Why did you feel hurt? Why, *mother?*"
I fumbled for words as I understood
what he meant when he had made

the will of God comment.

Who entered whose arms first
I cannot remember but soon
he was sleeping *like a baby*
in my arms. What a child!

The gift I had brought
I gave - the seamless tunic
woven with love
many moons earlier
and he kissed my hands
and we parted.

Did time stand still on that hillside?
No, it inexorably moved and pointed
to another hilltop, one that would
fulfil Simeon's prophecy entirely.

The much-loved itinerant preacher
suddenly became the black sheep
of the administration. His sermons,
they claimed, were incendiary,

rousing people against the state.
He had to go, he would be crushed.
I wondered, if it was for this
that I had brought him forth.
What good could his death bring?

That path to Golgotha
twisted and turned
in my mind for long after.

The final scenes unfolded
before my eyes, blurred
with pain and tears: my son
lurching under the weight
of a tree
that was to bear him,
as crowds lined up early in the morning
to watch this Roman spectacle.
The ones he healed and put right,
were they present there then?
The miracles he wrought
why were they suddenly forgotten?

Someone important, centurion,
they called him, was giving orders,
and I witnessed the disrobing,
my cheeks scarlet,
burning in shame; distress
and impotent rage engulfing my senses.

What followed was worse,
the nailing; my mind went numb
at the sight of long, rusty nails
piercing through bone and flesh.
The harsh sounds, the yells,
the cross being drawn up,
jerked this way and that,
then finally fixed,
the labored breathing, the hiccups,
and then the silence.

The day drew to a close
and yet it would not stop,
the churning in my heart,
as the rowdy soldiers
drew lots for my son's clothing,

They laughed and tossed it in the air;
a mere sport for them.
One soldier bent and picked it up,
dusted it and folded it;
the tunic without seam,
it had a new owner.

On that dusty, stony path uphill,
marked with his precious blood
a few faithful disciples alongside,
I had followed because I had wanted,
desperately wanted to see God,
his Father, pull off the impossible.
But that didn't happen.
And there he was, at the end, bloodied,
on my legs, as he had been at birth.
Only now lifeless.
What child indeed!

Did I weep? I don't remember.
Just that I felt glad deep down that
he had moved from pain and politics.
What would the future hold

without him living and breathing?
Hearing about him,
what people said of him, his miracles.
His loving gaze and his kindness.
All that was gone.

Hanging from the tree,
he entrusted me to the care of John.
Then breathed his last.

I was in a haze for three days,
The sword had found its mark
and gouged out a deep part
of my being.

Yet I felt strangely expectant,
like I was going to give birth again.
I didn't tell anyone, I couldn't have.
It was the same illicit feeling
all over again. How could a widowed mother
feel expectant all over again?

And so I pondered and pondered

till I remembered how
he had vanished from our midst
at age twelve, while returning from Jerusalem,
and how, when I had gently berated him,
he had said, "Didn't you know I'd be
in my Father's house?"

Those teenage years had been
quite a struggle
for me to understand
the way his mind worked.
We were a different kind of close, not one
where speaking and proximity was needed.

Even at that wedding feast at Cana,
so brusque had been his manner
when I asked him to help.
Still he obeyed. And I wondered all the more
about his dying. Was it
out of a deep sense of obedience after all?

The more I wandered
in the realm of my thoughts,

the more convinced I was that all was not over.
But what more could happen?

In the upper room, it was I
comforting the disciples, mothering them.
That's when I heard the women whisper,
aloes and myrrh, aloes and myrrh.
They were planning to go to the tomb
and complete the burial rituals
on the dawn of the third day.
Myrrh, an ointment to embalm,
triggered a memory I'd put away
from long ago,
the day the Magi from the East visited.
Such strange things they'd uttered,
I barely understood
as they paid homage
to my bonny babe, who gurgled
and drooled through it all.
I finally saw why they had gifted us myrrh.
But I still could not comprehend
the *reason* for such a terrible fate.
What mother could?

On Calvary,

when the Roman soldiers

finally allowed us closer to where

he hung on the cross, he was already

at the point of death. I was distressed

that I could do nothing

to ease his pain, or even touch him,

or shoo the birds that kept closing in.

Like him, I felt abandoned,

betrayed by the Most High.

And then, as his head lay motionless,

they came and tore out his side.

A deep sense of helplessness

overcame me then,

and I thought, it is finished.

It was on the third day,

only on the third day, that things

began looking up.

Sightings and garbled stories

by the women returning from the tomb,

and disciples running back from Emmaus.

Risen from the dead, there he stood in our midst,
"Peace be with you, " he breathed.
Oh, never was joy felt so intensely
as on that blessed day!
His suffering bore fruit,
the Father had a plan all along.

My Risen Son didn't speak to me directly or so
thought everyone. But we communicated,
I will honour you, He said,
You shall be blessed
among all women.
Tosh, I said lovingly. Feed my Lambs,
He said, indicating the disciples
intoxicated with new wine[5].
I smiled. I'd like to meet Simeon someday.

Epilogue

Time is of no essence now.

I will go back one day to my Maker,

and when he asks me for a reckoning,

I'll breezily say, I was MOTHER OF GOD,

and he'll wave me in just like that,

like long lost friends meeting again.

Notes

Zaccheus[1]

He is the much-despised tax-collector, a short man whom we meet in the Gospel of Luke. He is caught in a crowd of people thronging Jesus and cannot see the holy man. So he does the unthinkable for an adult man in those times. He runs ahead, climbs a tree and from his vantage point, waits for Jesus to pass by.

The Angel[2]

Traditionally the angel appearing to Mary with God's message of incarnation is considered to be Gabriel, one of the four Archangels. This story is found in the second chapter of Luke's Gospel.

Elizabeth[3]

Elizabeth and her husband, Zechariah are the older couple we meet in Luke's Gospel. Zechariah is from the priestly class of Levites. His wife, Elizabeth is ashamed of conceiving in her old age. What would have been considered old age for those times? It is safe to assume Elizabeth within the age range of 37-45. She has borne no children and is considered by those around her as barren. It is possible that, due to this fact, she and her husband were the target of many unkind remarks as barrenness was looked upon as a curse in those days. This probably got worse after her late-in-life conception. Hence her self-enforced reticence.

The reference to her husband's muteness is to point out his unbelieving stance when he has a vision while serving in the temple. He is informed that his wife will conceive when his period of service ends and he refuses to believe. The sign given to him is his sudden muteness, which lifts only when he affirms the name his wife gives to their son, John.

Joseph[4]

Joseph was betrothed to Mary, but, as the Gospel of Matthew informs us, before they came to live together, Mary was rumoured to be with child. The punishment for this – it was a crime to be an unwed mother by the Jewish standards of those times – was death by stoning.

35

Joseph wanted to spare Mary that fate and decided to divorce her privately. It must be noted here that 'betrothal' was treated as serious as marriage and is not to be confused with the common understanding of 'engagement' in today's times. Hence a betrothal could only be ended by a divorce. By marrying Mary who is with child, he officially becomes the adoptive father of her child, according to Jewish law of the time.

New Wine[5]

This term is used several times by Jesus in his discourses to refer to the Holy Spirit, the third person in the Christian understanding of a 'Trinitarian' God.

Acknowledgements

As author, I would like to acknowledge with deepest gratitude the persons who have made this publication possible.

My husband, Mahesh, whose unstinting support has seen me through the worst of times.

Mr Victor Rangel-Ribeiro, author of the much acclaimed novel based on Goan life, *Tivolim*, now settled in the US, who read my work and suggested edits and re-read the piece. I remain deeply obliged to him.

Third in order, but not necessarily in merit, the immense love and support of several writer friends in the GoaWriters group. They have continuously encouraged me and pushed me to write.

Book Excerpt

From *Healed of Chronic Hemorrhage*

The Prologue:

A vision shimmers before my eyes.

Desert mirage, I console myself.

A young girl newly married,

terrified and excited at being alone

with her husband,

finds the price of marriage too high.

Her body can't cope

with the insatiable demands

and slowly she curls up,

like a flower wilting.

This virgin doesn't conceive.

Others around her sprout

babies while she keeps count

of the days of her cycle:

ten, twelve, fifteen, nineteen…

The bleeding is a sign

that she's alive, though she'd

rather be dead.

It keeps him away.

For that she is glad.

But that also means

a darkened, hidden existence.

Life slips before her eyes,

swept away by a desert storm.

Now *she* remains,

the storm is gone.

Closer than a faithful friend

are the shackles

of the haemorrhage.

Now *she* remains

and *that* remains.

The mirage vaporises.

I shudder.

For so long I've kept

this part of my life buried,

the original source

of my gall, my sorrow.

I did not want any part in sorrow.

Anger was enough to carry me through,

or so I thought till my eyes met *His*.

(End of Excerpt)

Author Information

Ermelinda Makkimane has studied the Scriptures and Feminist perspectives in Literature. This gives her a unique hold over the topic she has written on – a womanist perspective on Mary.

Ms Makkimane loves thinking poetry and sometimes she writes down those words. She lives in a hamlet on the river island of Divar in Goa, India's tiniest state, where she spends a lot of time listening to bird calls and watching the afternoon breeze scandalise the leaves.

Ms Makkimane is currently working on the third book in the series "Her Story". The series aims to foreground some of the women characters of the New and Old Testaments, to give a voice to those women whose lives can only now be re-imagined.

Connect with the Author

Amazon Author Page:

https://www.amazon.com/author/ermelindamakkimane

Goodreads Author Page:

https://www.goodreads.com/author/show/20514902.Erm elinda_Makkimane

BookBub Author Page:

https://www.bookbub.com/profile/ermelinda-makkimane

Facebook Author Page:

https://www.facebook.com/ermelindamakkimaneauthorh erstory

Email:

ermelindamakkimane@gmail.com

Blog:

http://ermelindamakkimane.wordpress.com

Leave a one-click review!

Thank you for reading "Her Story." It would mean a lot if you could take a minute of your time to leave a review. It will help this independent author immensely and can be a few short sentences. Scroll down the page after you click below.

CLICK HERE

Printed in Great Britain
by Amazon

58348210R00028